Pins

Pins

Natalie Morrison

Victoria University of Wellington Press

Victoria University of Wellington Press
PO Box 600, Wellington
New Zealand
vup.wgtn.ac.nz

A catalogue record is available at the National Library of New Zealand

ISBN 9781776563036

Printed by Ligare, Auckland

for Valerie Grace

I found a cure, I found a cure, I found a cure to ease your pain.

—'Young Girls', PINS

Your obsession with pins
is my peculiar inheritance.

At first there is little light in the cellar.
Dust motes, dark mice, corners
and then the first heavenly glint
of the safety pin.

So, I remember you saying you felt stuck.
. . . *stuck in your mire, in your shit . . .*
Apparently, that's what sisters do.
After a tattoo your friend gave you at school
you spent hours curled in my bed; it still has
the print of your raw bicep,
your floral-negative.

A woman had one hundred pins
and losing one of them
to her floor, clotted
with dust, tried
to find it.

In the future, there will be a new procedure
for excavating the brain: faintest sliver of pin
about twenty centimetres in length,
so delicate that the surgeon's breath, like
the slight huff from a fridge door,
could snap it.

The woman in question has been looking
for her lost pin to this very day.

Some unfortunate pickpocket stole your photograph
out of a slit in my mother's wallet. It strikes me
as acutely characteristic of you; among strangers
you're perhaps a glint in passing, or stock-still on a bedside
table (a pretend girlfriend), or dizzying in a gutter whirlpool
after heavy rain.

One stranger turns to another on the train.
Each pin sits neatly with its peers.

Some of your favourite words:
brusque
burst
bask
brim
pin

I have begun to dedicate things to you.
These poems, for example; I pin snippets
to your bedroom wall.

Why do we look at the needle in our neighbour's eye
and pay no attention to the pin
in our own?

The photograph in the wallet:
with a chin like yours you'll never need
to be afraid. You were looking towards
the ceiling, the mound of your chin almost obscuring your eyes
made up like tar bubbles, your nineties hair spikes dipped red
for poison. You told me to stay away from the spikes.
I never came near you with balloons. I could see right up
into the cosmic blank inside each nostril.

Not many people realise that pins
inhabit the underworld
– a thing of beauty in the eye
of the beholder, a gleam of hellfire.

Before now, we never had a corkboard
for notices, flyers, crimped receipts.
I have formed the ridiculous habit
of removing pins when I pass the kitchen.
I squint into the holes.

How much are we an agent of the pin's removal?

The first thing you took with you:
elephant lapel pin, thumb-sized, grey
except for the terrified whites of its eyes.
When I told the detective sergeant this
she gave me a freshly laundered
sort of smile.

Exclamation mark: sudden disconnect
of the pin previously stuck in paper.
Extraordinary!

You didn't think I could ever name one hundred pins
without taking a breath.

The second thing you took with you:
The Lord of the Rings, the entire trilogy in paperback.
When our mum told us that the tiny holes in the pages
were not pinpricks at all but microscopic beetles,
you listened for the beetles when she left the room,
ear to the cover, to see if you could hear them chewing.

It is possible to read fortunes with a pin:
three pins are held between the lips and by
the angle at which they point away from the face,
one can tell whether the person will find true love.

In your edition you've exchanged the word 'ring'
for 'pin', an impressive alteration: in Tolkien's trilogy
the word 'ring' occurs 338 times.

I can just about trace the birth of your fascination.
We were cordoned off from the fireplace with a moveable
copper façade. Nana was stitching one of Grandad's
socks. We didn't have any clothes on,
were still dripping slightly from the bath.
You picked up a pinch of metal
and in the dim light tried to see what it was
you were holding. I continued reading Beatrix Potter
with a damp index finger. Nana told you to be careful:
What you have in your hand is very sharp.

Caution: where there is a pin
there will be puns.

One must love a sister in the same way one must love
jabbing oneself in the foot halfway up a flight of carpeted stairs.
Our parents told you I would be a nice surprise.

If all the pins in the world were gathered together they would fill 3000 Olympic swimming pools.

The rolling pin is perfect for flaky pastry. It weighs the same as a head going over the top.

The replacement wallet photo:
the photo was taken by Mum who
was walking behind us. You were
trailing my wrist as you stooped
into the car. It must have been the
winter highlights coming slant-wise
that made the elephant brooch
stick out like a sore point of starlight
from your jacket collar. It came out
in the photograph as a spot of bright
white. My own constellation spot
appears to come off the side of my
glasses. From the picture, one can't
make out your nails in the tender portion
of my inner wrist. Days later, I still had
the smiley face marks.

This is the ratio: the blue whale is to the human as
the party frock is to the pin.

The third thing you took with you:
frumpy yellow quilt. Nana was a mathematician
and the sewing of the quilt was her lasting lesson
to us about geometry. In the sun, the quilt
slowly turned albino with our love.

In 1995, you could get one hundred pins for less than two dollars.

You began to take Sundays a bit much to heart.
Our cousin's Action Man was found pinned
to a tree stump by the wrist and ankles. Next,
you woke me complaining of birth
pains on Christmas Eve.

Distinguishing feature:
large pin on a string against your chest.

I suppose we have the pin to thank for the invention of the punk.

Another distinguishing feature: a homemade tattoo,
upper arm, near the shoulder, rose petals
bunched at the wrong places.
From a few steps away
it becomes a bruise.

P
I
N
S
I
Z
E
D
S
O
N
N
E
T

It became a ritual, exchanging the worst possible
deaths we could imagine while brushing our teeth.
Number nine involved pins.

The greatest joy in life is purchasing a new box set
of pins. They have been holding their factory-packaged breath
until now. Ready for a life of petty crime.

You kept saying you were going to live at Nana's house,
do the tricky bits of her quilting that her fingers
got stuck with these days – her knuckles
less knuckle, more stumps of white coral.

Glossary of Illegal Terms:
pincredible
pindignation
pinstrument
pinevitable
pinvisible
pinvincible
pinfrastructure
pintuition
pinformation
pinnuendo

For a month you were banned from mentioning the word.
Like an amputee coaxing a ghost leg up the stairs,
you talked to me non-stop about your 'sharp objects'.

Our mother's clearest sign of affection:
chasing us through the overgrown back of the garden
pretending to be a rhinoceros, wearing a rose thorn
on the tip of her nose.

Our father's clearest sign of affection:
unrolling sleeping bags on the lawn after dark and
smoking under the stars as he pointed some of them out.
That's your one. The one next to that is your sister's.
We had been exchanging blows only a moment ago
about the stars we pinned to the star chart every week.
Sometimes his knee would block my view or stars would
intermittently disappear behind spurts
of cirrus cloud from his chin.

Number nine, your favourite:
a swimming pool filled with pins for the Olympics
and afterwards a metallic corpse.

Assignment due 1 November (4 credits):
Using only materials found around your house – e.g. magazines,
ornaments, paperclips, pins – create an art installation
which draws on this year's theme of 'connection'.
In your scrapbook folios record the process of creating this installation with
photographs of your work and a discussion on . . .

A prank you especially savoured was the one where
you waited until I had started to twitch in my sleep
before pricking me in the palm of my hand.
I demanded separate rooms.

Our priorities were worlds apart; you'd rather
not go to the zoo on the perfect day for it,
but you heard the 'pin' in tenpin bowling.
Sensing the tip of your bad mood, Mum
steered us through to the bowling alley,
in which I would stand for hours in the half light
nursing my copper ball baby, triple-eyed. I felt sure
I was going to drop it on my little toe.

Camouflage:
the pin has evolved in such a way
as to baffle the most hawk-eyed of predators.

Now that all these pieces have been pinned
I can turn three hundred and sixty degrees and see them all.
Eventually, we'll take them down. Your wallpaper
a wide display of open pores.

There is nothing more piercingly clear
than a sister who does not want to return home.

Public Information Notice
Post-It Note
Prostatic Intraepithelial Neoplasia
Parent Information Night
Personal Identity Number
Pain in the Neck

You were always first in line for the flu jab.

Every time you pierced an ear
(in the back shed, with the rats)
you would bring home another boyfriend.
You said it was a knee-jerk reaction.

On several occasions, I have walked in on my mother
reading your school reports. Look at this:
a smiley, exuberant member of the class.
This is how *I* would write your school reports:
a smiley, exuberant wielder of pins.

Your answer to my question about heartburn:
a sharp pain in the chest.

Give a man a pin
                and he will prick himself for a week.

Your wardrobe is the space I like best. I'm surprised
by what you chose to leave behind. Your jacket
drapes a casual arm over my shoulder. I pretend
you are fastening a lapel pin, absurdly
from behind, *all the better to prick you with
my dear.*

A barcode: tight-knit family of pins.

After breaking his shin bone in a cycling accident,
our dad had a pin put in to hold the bones
together. You spent a whole afternoon
staring at his leg as though you could see
right the way through.

The pinwheel girl takes up most
of the poster. Mellow spring lambs look on
at her, nauseous with envy. They watch
her pinwheel flick and flick the paper or
plastic curls around, when she makes wind go
through a gap in her front teeth.

For a while, we treated you like a lost cat.
Have you seen this girl? Please contact.
Red-rimmed signs and posts by the road
watched us as we pinned up forests.

Bend an ear to an elderly lump of newsprint on an old desk.
Hark the paper cricket, its faint chirrup from amongst the pages.
The paper cricket is distinguishable from the common thumbtack
by the startling birdlike quality of its song.

The seam will not mend itself. A single pin cannot fix this.

Mum would say goodnight to me
and then to your bedroom walls (pins in the dark
wallpaper). Eventually it wore her down.

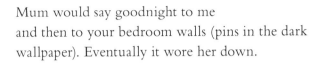

When reaching into a sewing box, be prepared
to lift out a lacerated hand.

The online personality test kept insisting you were fated
to be a little mermaid with bright red hair. You pinched
up your face, clicking and clicking with rising ferocity.
What you wanted was to be asleep for a thousand years,
slumped under a spindle.

Only a handful of people will have a dream about a pin-like object
during their lifetime.

Nana explained about the dawn
being the point at which the fabric strains at the seams
and where the thin-tacked horizon pulls free, fraying
– that is where you first see the sun.

Nana, reaching for her thimble,
said she didn't know about sunsets.

You tried to illustrate your unusual dream to me
by sticking a triangle of pins in your wall.
Look, you said, *it was like this:*
in my dream I couldn't look away.

Pigeons know nothing about pins.
Literally nothing.

Consider what might be going through a pigeon's mind when
a pin is placed in front of it in a controlled laboratory
environment:
animal?
vegetable?
obstacle?

Be suspicious
of any injuries obtained in the presence of a pin.

Mrs Alan calls me [your name]
and when I look back down at my hands,
there is a tiny red bauble perched
on my thumb. I think, *for the ants,*
their Christmases have come. I'm sure
you would have said the same.
Blood sugar level
and all that.

If all the pins in the world were put tip to tip in a vertical
stack, they would reach all the way to the moon and back.

Casper whines to be let inside. He slides his nose along
the bottom of the stained glass. His nose becomes a piglet's snout,
twin curls of cartilage sucking in and out. We would laugh at him
when we were told not to laugh. Once, he came indoors
with a hedgehog spine sticking out of his nose. You laughed
so hard that pee ran out in an oval pool on your seat.

Because of your early enchantment with fairy stories,
I wasn't surprised to pick up your trail of bobby pins
along the footpaths of Wellington's suburbs. I imagined
finally arriving at your gingerbread destination.

Our parents let you keep them in a box:
bayonets for bottle-green artillerymen or
fine silver toothpicks for our lady-banquets
during which we would consume
the dainty limbs of crane flies
and microscopic rice cakes.

While we waited at Nana's place we amused ourselves
with the pincushion, taking it in turns to lower our hand
onto the welcome delight of robot hair. You would raise your voice
like hackles whenever we heard, from the phone call in the next room,
the words 'home' or 'can't stay here forever'.

Your bedroom has a tendency for dampness now because
no one goes in there. Mum leaves your window open.
Curtain held back with a thumbtack.

The inventor of the safety pin couldn't stand
his recurring dreams concerning
porcupine quills
bee stings
forests of green needles.

I find your birthday cards piled
in your underwear drawer. Mum writes:
You were an embryo no bigger
than the head of a pin.

Head:
Please find attached.
Sincerely,
The Pin Manufacturer

Length:
Euclid described a line
as a 'breadthless length'.

Breathless, I tug a line
between this pin
and the next.

Thickness:
Mum makes soup every other day,
mainly for the splintery strep in her throat,
also for your potential entrance
through our dark blue
corridor.

Metal Content:
A pin held in the teeth leaves a bitter tang,
same as the word tinnitus.

Point:
Dad drove you home. *How many times
do you expect me . . . ?* He dropped the thought
as he came to the next intersection. His other thoughts tossed
heavily in the glove box, hardboiled. *You're so dramatic,* he said.
You teared up watching the car's speedometer lift
its one shaky limb.

Pine needle tea apparently
tastes like the bite
of a crab-apple.

'I cannot keep the pin and stay here. I ought to leave everything and go away.'
– Frodo, page sixty-one of your edition.

First encounter:
Mum convinced me to take myself to the local primary school gala. There are only so many ways you can walk around a local school gala by yourself without appearing conspicuous. One technique is to join lines. I was in line for the dart throwing, but I couldn't see what the darts were being directed at. Whatever it once had been, it was now shredded past the point of recognition. The papery eyes, mouth and the entirety of the chin had given way to the light brown corkboard beneath. More people joined the queue and the person behind me tried to start up the school song, or rather the tune of the school song with a slurry of odd words. It was almost my turn. To get my wallet out of my shoulder-bag I had to twist around. It wasn't your face that caught my eye in the end. Because I was bent down, the elephant lapel pin on your chest met me at eye-height as I swivelled for my loose change. But before I could open my mouth, you'd already gone. That was you sprinting from the school grounds, faux military boots hammering into the mud.

The photographs that have you in them quiver
in my hand. On their journey towards the wall
they catch sight of the pins
on the windowsill.

There is a fine line between
Barbie doll acupuncture and Barbie doll voodoo.

Telling our mum was almost the same
as telling the soup that I saw you.
The soup was on LOW.
Mum's face was hovering over the soup,
seasoning. The soup is her kind of world
on slow rotation, spoon milling on its axis.
The soup said it was very interested in seeing you
again, stifling a heartfelt sniff.
Mum slid her fingernail from side
to side on the bench top, inadvertently tracing
the unsightly indent of a pin.

For the prize, how many pins are in this jar?

Your collection ranges from a regular
spring-pin, possibly twisted out of some wheel or other
at the bread factory, still tinged swamp-black,
to an elegant eighteen-inch Victorian
hat-pin.

When I think of your brain, I think
not of neurons, or anything remotely organic,
cells stretching limb to limb. Instead,
I think of a clump of magnetised
sewing equipment. You brainy
hedgehog you.

On the way to visiting the Weta Cave, a few
suburbs over, you were finally faced with the most
magnificent pin you'd ever seen.
Its tip had been bandaged up
in duct tape after being struck by lightning.
We were edgy about your potential disappointment,
but you stood there looking up, soaking your shaggy
woollen penguin jumper right through. It was
a striking installation, the metal shard so large
it would bow across the highway in the wind.

Drop one pin into a glass of clear
cold water for several minutes.
Then immerse your hand in the language
of the water until you find it.

Second encounter:
You'd obviously got your hands on a violin.
I caught sight of you fiddling with its wonky pins
by the doorway to the pet shop. Your hands
bracing the body of the decrepit thing appeared blue
in the cold against the violin's bright yellow paint.
Without seeing I was there, you lifted the bow
to the bridge and a sour twang began shivering.

In some cases, a very small insect
may be speared through the thorax by a minuten pin.

Rest Home:
Our mum shifts Nana off her easy chair, they go all the way
to the window in seven jaunty paces. Mum jabs the window
that looks onto the garden, the hedgerows with leaves
like a thousand slick manicures. *There isn't even a window
to open*, Mum says. Nana sways dubiously
with each bracketed step back towards her easy chair.
You probably dreamt that she was there.

Sure enough, her rest home had been having 'security issues'.
I blame the girl with the pin.

An antidote for bad teeth is to open cloves
with the molars like splitting one
tough-roasted nut or a fairy's skull.
An antidote for sister-itis is to crackle the tiniest
of her pins between the affected teeth.

Legend has it that Nana
only ever used the term 'pinhead' to describe our dad.

I am reading *The Hunger Games*
because it's all the rage. I imagine
you would be so jealous
of Katniss Everdeen sporting her
mockingjay pin that you'd shred up
the inside of your own cheek.

I began to think that I'd only ever encounter you in glimpses
from now on, like binoculars intermittently lifted
to my eyes. I know for a fact that birdwatchers
don't actually twitch, but rather
they drop into their open eyes, silently, as if the bird
held their heart-pin, ready to pull it out at any moment.

It sounds clock-like. Of midnight. Of arms passing
over and over in an aquatic centre. We are in a medical
centre. The Pinhead is wearing his new bedside manner.
Nana says:
Dad says: *I didn't quite catch that.*
Nana says:
Dad says: *I didn't quite catch that.*

Protective equipment against the pin:
hard hat
goggles
PVC rain coat
thimble

I have taken the liberty of scratching [your name]
into the desks at school over and over so
after all this time, the teachers might still
believe it was you.

Here is proof of your goodness:
after the dead gorse had embedded itself
in the heel of my hand following
a skid on the track to the beach, you
latched on with your black lipsticked mouth,
caught the end of the prickle in your teeth.

Mechanical pin:
point around which the mechanism rotates.

Why was it that we always pictured you
coming in through the windows? The drawing pin
that had been holding your curtain fell
on the floor directly under the windowsill
where I watered the aloe vera sprout.
Like all pins must, it got a hold of me by the middle toe.

At the edge of consciousness,
those who are fortunate enough to see it
will discover three pins, triangulated
jabbed into a green-apple-skin wall.
They will be at a loss
to explain this phenomenon:
is this holy?
is this the luck of the third try?
is this the beginning?
the middle? the end?
is this a joke?
is this the thing we never dare to say?

Since the 1960s it has been standard medical practice
to prick a newborn in the heel of its foot.
The newborn will scream louder and longer
than anyone else in the room.

We have Australian friends
to dinner. This goes fine
until we find that the wife is addicted
to Sudoku and she asks the room
for a 'pen'.
The dining table is silent.

Nana cannot concentrate on a pin any longer
than several seconds now before the thin glow-
line of it wavers and her over-rubbed attention
returns to us.

A pluton hovering on the outskirts
like one pin among the solar system's
collection of silvery thumb tacks.

Hail:
walking into a downpour of a thousand brisk pins.

Hail (alternative theory):
all the angels in heaven empty their sewing kits at once,
perhaps in protest. Perhaps in the name of equal rights.

I could barely find my way around
your bedroom floor without piercing my foot.
All the bits of paper and pins which were
seemingly random, seemingly momentous.

If the silver pin whistles
then tomorrow there will be rain.

Nana closes the lid on the conversation, convoluted
as it is. Nicotine traces back through the church
from the foyer where our father is pinching his cigarette
(for the road). On his side of the building, the limp stub
is flattened in the middle, he's holding so tight.
On her side, she quietly curses him for smoking indoors,
she can smell it from all the way over here, it leaks
under the lid, through the slots of artificial light.
Her box will *not* be contaminated.
In the intervening pews, I shuffle a new playlist into my ear.
Mum is off laminating memorial pictures of Nana's grin
somewhere. I have the hymns coming round
my head in waves and I wonder where I might discreetly
throw up. One elderly male in a toffee shirt is saying his
goodbyes in Catholic. Perhaps he is my long-lost grandfather
after all these years. There is now – give or take
– one hour and fifty minutes before the cremation.
I brought her pincushion and an assortment of pins
on your behalf, as a sign of respect. My hands look like a cat
got them, Nana's wicker sewing kit was such a mess,
you wouldn't believe. Taking them from my bag now,
as your humble representative, I place the pincushion
on the pew and proceed to drive the ends in.
By the time I've finished, they're all standing to attention.

Throughout the emerging garment
the seamstress's pinch and slip.

Nana's rubber thimble –
a knobbly teat of red skin.

At birthday parties, which always have too many fairies,
the donkey pinned to the wall has the least fun.

Certain hotels will provide a complimentary sewing kit.
You used to pick out the pins like some other child might
eagerly pluck the black jellybeans.

In the days leading up
to your proper departure,
Casper tracked your every move,
pinned to you. Shove him off,
he'd leap right back up again
next to you on the bed. Prise
your arm from your side
with his head, getting his ears
squished. He'd prop his chin on your thigh
and sniff for the longest time.

After telling him what you'd
been compelled to do, Dad ruffled
the neck of the dog with an absent hand.
At seven o'clock his stubble had stuck wires
through his chin like the back of a corkboard.
Pick yourself up, brush yourself
off and move on. His opinion,
not mine. Whistled across the mouth
off his Speight's bottle and, of course,
that day you decided to finally take his advice.

A solemn hand signal:
to remove the pin from the top
and throw.

As I searched for a satisfactory picture
of a burrowing owl to add to my Pinterest
board, an article caught my eye about
dogs that can sense the presence
of human embryos
even through layers and layers.

With every job that must be done
there is an element of surprise.
A pin, its sabotage.

Such an unexpected contact:
On a road trip north, I found myself standing in Marton's only
secondhand bookstore with your copy of *The Lord of the Rings*
drooping slightly in my hands. You must have dipped your head
through this very doorway.
My neck hairs began to
point in all your
directions.

Am I the secondhand sister?
Am I the paper-doll daughter?
They are sticking through me –
silver points appear out of my back.

My PIN number:
★★★★

Microsoft's *Pinball* is supposed to be set in space.
Who knew the universe could make
such exciting noises!

On rare occasions, one member of the Mafia
will send another a pin in a plain envelope licked shut
with the sender's personal spit, to signify new life.

The moment I decided to use your pins
for my art installation I knew you
would hate me for it.
That moment coincided with
an absence of blood in my arm.
I had to return my arm to my side
with my other hand. Had you filled my arm
with sand in my sleep, I wouldn't have been surprised.
My arm your new joke, your sausagey doorstop.

Ecstasy is happiness at its highest volume.
A pain in the wrist is a pin magnified 300x.

I'm still trying to decide what you wanted to say.
Several days after my birthday, Mum flicked through the mail
and stopped. Your spelling wasn't exemplary, in fact
not much had changed since your ruined spelling book, your Ps
making Qs. Whenever you wrote my name, people got choked up.
On the front of the envelope, you'd written in sharpie pen
for optimum effect, squiggled the address. A tissue, the kind you pull
at public toilets, had in its folds your astonished elephant,
that single pin.

After years of curling up to the tune of Bob Dylan's 'Oh Sister',
the point making its rounds along that vinyl groove, I was told
that the lyrics might actually be about sex.
I will not believe it.

At one point in the night I hear our dad leave his bed.
Once outside, he switches the torch from shed
to hedge to hedge and all along the fence.
He only says
[your name]
once.
My walls can
just about decipher
him, his shadow. He dips in
and out of focus like a teabag
in milky water. When he comes back, the insides
of the house are all around him.

Pins in the bath, sleek:
these are our dolphins slipping
in the watery ambience.

Oh sister, when the song dips round again
and I'm stuck in my apron, shaving deli ham
there is nothing I can do but twist, and lick shut
with sticky tape – New World red. Wait for Bob Dylan
to pass me by for the third time that morning. The overhead
tubes highlight the thermometer fresh dug into the mound
of corned beef.

What is the pin like from one to ten?
One being nothing at all and
ten being the biggest pin you've ever experienced.

You are the kind of girl who jumps in front of exclamation marks
valiantly.

The detective sergeant smiled and I could smell
the detergent spittle on her teeth. When she turned side-on I tried
to see behind the front of her black-blue plastic badge.

Dylan reminds me
of the lump in my bed, always
the right-hand side.
Mum had been uppity. You had
nearly liquored yourself
into hibernation.
Leaning over you to
turn out the bedside lamp shaped
like my favourite owl,
you stopped me midway
across. Reached a hand into
my hair and pulled out my
hairclip with a strand
still attached. You said
magic trick. We always
differentiated; you had pins
and I had clips. You pointed
out how the hair curved
upwards like a pencil tick.

The final touches were making themselves felt in the last days
of my art assignment. It was all about clearing room for each bit
as it came, and by torchlight I tacked the last piece on the corner
closest to your wardrobe, near the skirting boards.
The pin I chose was small and grey with an enamel trunk
bent up at the end from snagging on other people's clothes.

But I will always have you in the back of my mind,
unwinding like the coil pin in the body of a bright,
jittery, copper toy.

If all the pins in the world were gathered together
you would be very much pleased.
But all the pins in the world
cannot be gathered
together.

Oh sister, I recognise your stoop everywhere.
After trying not to learn to play Nana's piano
you developed that characteristic lack
of posture. It didn't help that you spent hours
bum to floor, peering into your pin box
like the three fairies must have peered into the shaded
cradle. Whenever I cross the road I peer under the rain
jacket hoods of people going in the opposite direction.

Almost all of our road trips:
I spy with my little eye something beginning with P.

Oh sister, I catch you in the corner of my eye like a splinter of sleep.
You are level with the electro-magnetic detectors either side, like
two hands about to clap. Your hoodie ducks under
the exit sign before the automatic doors.
I watch your back.

The pin can slip into a crowd
seamlessly.

When I am the no one
who enters your room
to pin these poems
to your wall, I find
a great swirl of moths.

Notes

The characters in this poem are fictional. To my knowledge, none of my sisters harbour a pin obsession.

The epigraph used in this book was taken from lyrics of the song 'Young Girls' from the 2015 album *Wild Nights* by the English rock band PINS.

Some segments of Pins were published in *Takahē* 86 magazine in 2016 as 'Seven Hundred Ways of Looking at a Pin'.

On page 37, the definition of a line was taken from *Elements* (book 1, definition 2) by Euclid of Alexandria.

I refer to *The Lord of the Rings* trilogy by J.R.R. Tolkien on page 13 and 39. On page 39, the quote from *The Fellowship of the Ring* has been altered from 'I cannot keep the ring and stay here'.

Acknowledgements

Victoria University Press, I want to thank you times a million! Ashleigh Young, thank you for your thoughts and edits. You have been extremely kind with your time and reassurance.

James Brown, thank you for your most detailed attention to this poem as my MA supervisor; what would have become of these pins without your feedback, suggestions and enthusiasm? My gratitude to Chris Price for her expert guidance and feedback while this poem was growing up.

Hearty thank-yous to the lovely creatures of MA 2016, especially: Paula, Hannah, Evangeline, Cherie, William, Rebecca, Kirsti, Vivienne and Kerry. Each of you inspired and shaped this book. I miss our afternoons together.

Mary and Peter Biggs, your generosity allowed me some breathing space to work on this poem. Thank you both.

I am so grateful for the patience and understanding of my flatmates who've lived with me through a blizzard of pins. Thank you members of the Semeloff Practical Ladies Club, and Laura and Andrew Loach.

I reserve the ultimate thanks for my family and my partner, Francis. You have all supported me with such love, always.